Dedication

MW00443200

Evan James was born at 4:47 p.m. on December 19 – a Christmas baby.
Our 1st grandchild and life hasn't been the same!
He weighed 8 pounds and 10 ounces.
He was 20 inches long and had lots of dark hair.

This book is dedicated to Evan with tons and tons of love.

Acknowledgements

My heartfelt thanks to:

◊ *John Wagner, whose head, heart, and hands created these amazing illustrations*

◊ *Michele Stewart, whose editing gifts helped my ideas flow SO much better*

◊ *Nancy Winkler whose talent and patience laid out this wonderful "Big Surprise"*

◊ *Pat (wife) and Kelsey (daughter) Gareau for their relentless support and encouragement to write*

Copyright 2014

by Brian Gareau

Introduction

This is a "family" book and it's intended to be read to and with children. The book's goals are simple but powerful:

- Invest a little "quality time" to nurture a stronger relationship with a child.

- Model what matters! Listening, imagining, laughing, and reading are ALL important.

- Piggyback this story into your own. A special D.I.Y. is included at the end of the book.

So grab those bubbling, bundles of curiosity, energy and unimaginable joy. Find a comfy chair. Snuggle up. Together, find out the BIG SURPRISE.

Blessings,
Brian (aka Papa)

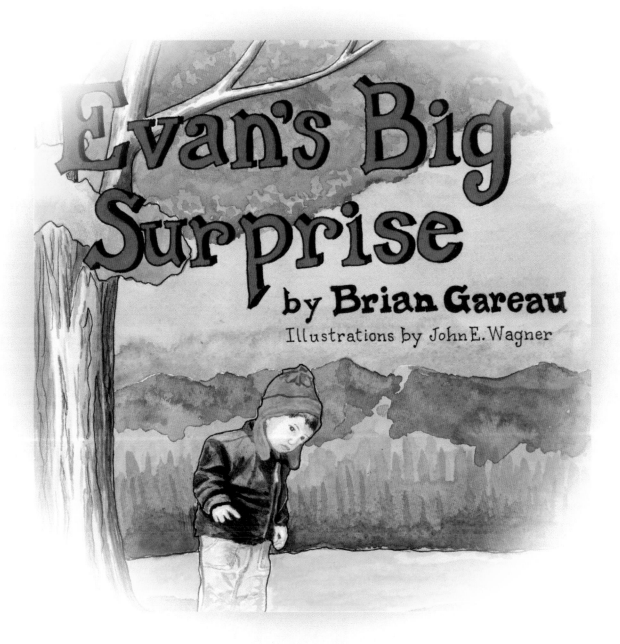

Evan's Big Surprise

by Brian Gareau

Illustrations by John E. Wagner

It was a bright, crisp fall day. Evan's Papa sat on the back deck deep in thought - 'doodling' in his head. Evan's birthday was only a few weeks away and Papa wanted to give him a BIG SURPRISE! What would it be?

Papa started thinking about all the M and M's he and Evan enjoyed together. But Papa's M and M's were not made of chocolate — although he and Evan loved those too. Papa's M and M's stood for "Making Memories" - those amazing, life time images and feelings in our head and heart that never melt away. Wonderful M and M's flashed through Papa's mind.

Then he pulled out his iPhone and looked at all of his pictures of Evan. Two pictures "jumped out."

"That's it!" shouted Papa. "Now I know what to do!"

Papa sent a text message to Evan's Daddy and Uncle. It read, "Working on a BIG SURPRISE for Evan's birthday. I could really use your help!"

Over the next several weeks, Evan's Papa, Daddy and Uncle would sneak out into the garage after Family Dinner Night. Everyone else would stay inside and keep Evan distracted from the noises, smells and laughter coming from the garage. No one ever peeked under the big blanket because Papa posted a warning sign.

Finally, it was Evan's birthday. Everyone was very excited. But, when the blanket was removed there was nothing there — just a special map Papa had drawn. The BIG SURPRISE had been moved out back.

Evan saw it first, in the big oak tree - an AMAZING, SUPER-DUPER bird feeder. He squealed!

"Hope you like it, little buddy", said Papa.   He reached down and Evan jumped in his arms.

The bird feeder was made of wood but it looked just like one of Papa's boots — only bigger. A long, clear tube with tiny openings and perches ran down the back of the feeder. This is where the thistle went for the very small birds. There were also cut outs on each side of the boot and the toe, where larger birds could eat their food. A wire mesh container, shaped like the letter "E", hung underneath and held suet for all the birds.

Next, Papa showed Evan three special buttons. Each time Evan pushed one, he heard a recording of Papa asking him what that bird said and his reply. Everyone laughed when they heard Evan's bird sounds of "Honk – Honk" (Goose); "Quack – Quack" (Duck); and "Tweet-Tweet (Finch)."

"There are some more special things to show you," said Papa. "Let's put some bird seed in the feeder."

Papa lifted a small cover at the top of the boot. Evan began pouring a small cup of bird seed into the built-in funnel. Little bells jingled as the seeds hit them. Evan's mouth made a big "O" and his eyes did too.

Finally, Papa opened a secret compartment in the bottom of the heel. Evan's Daddy and Uncle looked surprised because they didn't even know about it. Papa had been very sneaky – but in a good way. Inside was a small container and a hand-written note. Papa bent down and looked deeply into Evan's eyes. He said, "Your Momma and Daddy can read this to you now. But, hopefully, you will read it yourself many times as you grow up."

The note said:

Evan:

I hope you love your BIG SURPRISE. It was SO much fun to make for you. You are an amazing gift to our family. We thank God every day for sharing you with us.

We have spent a lot of special times sitting on our deck watching the birds. You get so excited every time we see one as they fly quickly from tree to tree. I also love all the different bird sounds you make.

As you grow up – your bird friends and I want to share some very important "life-long reminders" with you.

Blue Jays aren't actually blue, their feathers are brown. Light passes through their feathers causing us to see blue. Remember – Don't judge people by what you see on the outside. It's what's in their heart that counts the most.

Cardinals are fiercely defensive of their nests. Remember — Always defend your faith, family, values and home.

Chickadees are easily identified by the sounds they make. Remember – people will recognize you more by what you <u>do</u> than the noise you make.

Finches prefer to stick together in flocks. Remember – Your family is your flock. Always stick together even when there are disagreements and disappointments.

Hummingbirds are the only bird that can fly forwards and backwards. Remember – Sometimes in life you will need to take a step back before moving forward.

Woodpeckers don't get headaches from pecking. Remember – You <u>will</u> get a headache (physically or emotionally) if you keep hitting your head against a wall.

Finally, never ever forget the promise found in Isaiah 40:30-31. It's about a bird we do not have in our back yard — an **Eagle**. The Scripture says, "But those who wait upon God get fresh strength. They spread their wings and soar like eagles."

Evan didn't understand much of Papa's note just yet. But all at once his twinkling eyes caught Papa's and he made his sign language for "I love you" across his chest. Papa returned the sign - because birds of a feather always flock together.

Evan shouted, "HAPPY, HAPPY!"

Now It's Your Turn!

The page to the right has been left for you to personalize. Try one or more of the following ideas or make up your own. Share with the special children in your life, some of those important "life-long reminders." Leave a little legacy! Consider sharing:

- Where you were and your reaction when they were born

- How you came up with their nickname

- Songs and books you enjoyed together

- Favorite photos of them and your special memories

- Favorite recipe you like making for or with them

- Favorite conversations (like Evan's bird sounds)

- Special "M and M's" (making memories) you have had with them

- Important life lessons you hope they remember

- Favorite sayings, quotes, or scriptures that remind you of them

Brian's Biography

Brian Gareau is the proud father of three children. He became a Papa for the first time in 2012. He is blessed with a truly amazing wife and family! Brian is a keynote speaker, consultant, coach, and author. For more information on Brian's other books and services, visit his website at BrianGareauInc.com.

Crittenton Center's Crisis Nursery

We are blessed in our community to have a very special non-profit organization. The Crisis Nursery provides child abuse prevention services through emergency intervention and temporary care, crisis counseling and supportive services to families. It is open 24-hours, 7-days a week and all services are free. There are over 6000 admissions annually.

We are proud to donate 10% of all the earnings from this book to this exceptional organization. For more information see www.crittentoncenters.org

How to Order this Book

Copies of Evan's Big Surprise can be ordered on Amazon.com. For large book orders (25+), keynotes and workshops, contact Michele Lucia at michele@briangareauinc.com.

54768104R00025